Published by Lift Bridge Publishing
Copyright © 2015 by Ikisha Walker
All Rights Reserved
Library of Congress Cataloging-in-Publication Data
Walker, Ikisha.
#Confessionsofamother
Book Cover artist: Natasha Miller
ISBN 978-0-9961536-0-7
PRINTED IN THE UNITED STATES OF AMERICA
SECOND EDITION

Dedication

This book is dedicated to my earthly Trinity:

MY MOTHER (My Rock) DR.VELERIA L. COLEY

MY GRANDMOTHER (My Confidant) MOTHER MIRIAM L. MCKIVER

AND MY GODMOTHER (My Cheerleader) DR. SHARON STYLES-ANDERSON

THANK YOU FOR SPEAKING LIFE TO ME, OVER ME AND CONCERNING ME, WHEN I COULDN'T, I LOVE YOU FOREVER

KISHA

Foreward

The Blessing of a Child! What does that mean? Well, it all depends on YOUR definition. Ikisha is my eldest daughter who I had a hard time raising because I did not understand what I had and who she was. Why? Because no one told me who I was and how valuable I am! I was raised by a loving grandmother who not only showed me love but taught me how to love to the best of her ability. I took what I understood and used it with my children. Of course I made a bunch of mistakes because of ignorance, and with Ikisha it was really on the job training, therefore I didn't how to confess good things over her life; I was simply trying to survive, but as I allowed Jesus to teach me according to His word I began to do what I understood and gradually began to speak LIFE over my child! Now what makes sense is that when you began to speak Life over your children, you think that things begin to look better, but on the contrary I learned that as I began speaking LIFE over my children things got worse and I did not understand that the reason things got worse was because GOD HEARD ME and the devil was fighting to keep them as they were! As a mother you never want to see your child in a bad state for any reason, but sometimes bad things have to happen to get the good in them to come out! Romans 8:28 states that ALL things work together for the good of them who love God and who are the called according to His purpose! It takes a moment to accept ALL THINGS, but when you have a relationship with Christ it becomes easier to accept! Jesus told Simon Peter in Luke 22:31-32, Simon, Simon, behold Satan hath desired to have you, that he may sift you as wheat. But I have prayed for thee, that thy faith fail not: and when thou art converted, strengthen thy brethren.

#Confessionsofamother are so important to a mother, because when confessions come out of her mouth things began to happen! Ikisha believes what she is saying over her child, just like I believed and STILL believe what I spoke over her, and because of this belief manifestations are occurring and will continue to occur! Now what I've learned is they don't always occur the way we speak it but they still occur! Always remember that you will have what you say!

#Confessionsofamother will give SOMEONE (not just mothers) the God given ability and confidence to speak well over their children/families, breaking generational curses, speaking new and great ideas into their lives, etc. This book is my prayers coming to fruition and I didn't understand what or how God was going to do what HE does to get the glory but obvious this is one way! I am very humbled and proud to say that Jesus saw fit to use MY child to be a blessing to others!

CONTINUE TO SPEAK LIFE AND LIFE WILL COME, Kanye said "THIS IS THE GOOD LIFE!!" BUT JESUS SAID "I AM THE WAY, TRUTH AND THE LIFE!!!"

ONE MORE THING!!! NEVER CONFESS OVER YOUR CHILD WHAT SOMEONE ELSE THINKS THEY SHOULD BE UNLESS THEIR CONFESSIONS MATCH YOURS! Amen!

I love you!
Mommy

Let Us Pray...

Father I thank You for the opportunity to share what you've given me. I pray that every person that reads this book is blessed and empowered. I pray the every confession in this book is spoken with Power and with Conviction. I pray that every mother and father that speaks these confessions over their children BELIEVE IT!!!! That they are not just words, but declarations, proclamations, AND ANNOUNCEMENTS!!! I pray that every word that is spoken will not only take root in the child but root in the person who spoke these Words. Father, I pray that no person that comes in contact with this book remains the same. Father I thank You for these life changing Words. I pray that your power is in every single word in this book. I pray that Your Power rest where ever these words are spoken. I pray that Your Presence is felt when these words are spoken. God provoke change through this book, Allow restoration to come from this book, allow love to be resurrected from this book, allow your peace to come through this book. I pray for every mother that reads this book. I pray that you are strengthened; I pray that you are helped, I pray that you are healed and that your children are healed. I pray that the eyes of your understanding are open; I pray that this book blesses you; I pray these confessions take root in you and you BELIEVE the things that you're confessing over your child. I pray that you understand that the power is in your mouth to speak life over your child. I pray that your faith is increased; I pray that your love is increased; I pray that your compassion is increased and I pray that your defenses are increased, not against their fathers, but against the enemy of their souls. I pray that you find a middle ground with the father. I pray that you forgive him and release him from your spirit and from his mistakes. I pray that you allow him to be apart of their child's life, if that's his desire. I pray for every father that will read this book, I pray for the Uncles that will read this book, I pray for every godfather that will read this book, every grand father that will read this book, every mentor that will read this book, Allow every man that reads this book to gain courage and are encouraged to continue to strive to me the best role models that they can be for the children that are watching them. I pray for every absentee father that has no relationship with his children, I pray that this book will cause you to make a mends with your child and fight to be apart of their lives. YOUR SONS AND DAUGTHERS NEED YOU!!! Father I thank you in advance for every life that will be changed. I thank you for the trial that birth this book. I am thankful that you trusted me with the trial. I am grateful. Bless this CONFESSOR NOW!!! In Jesus Name Amen!!!

NOW SPEAK!!!

ISW

In the middle of giving birth you never think that when your child is born that they would be faced with so many different trials. The mere fact that they are born is an overwhelming and sometimes scary experience, the reality sets in that you now have a beautiful healthy baby that you have to provide for and protect. On Tuesday March 15th, 2005, I was blessed to give birth to a beautiful, healthy, bouncing baby boy, who weighed 8lbs 4oz; we named him Will Matthew "Judah". I had never known a love like this. I was amazed that I was the portal that God had chosen to bring him into this world, but I was also very afraid. How would I provide for him? How would I protect him from LIFE? I was very much aware of how special he was; I just didn't know the magnitude of the impact that he will have in the earth. I just knew that I wanted him to be the best person that he can be and I knew I needed God's help to ensure that he would be.

So here it is 9 years later, my once sweet little baby has grown into a very sweet still, but angry little boy, missing essential components that will contribute greatly to his growth as a young man. When he was born I was married to his father and due to life's circumstances, we are now divorced; now I am a single mother, raising this wonderful boy, who feels cheated by life and God because he doesn't have his dad. As a mother, it is gut-wrenching heart ache to see your only child struggle with self-worth and identity because of the absence of the other part of him, at least that's how he would try to explain it to me. Then I was faced with diagnoses, that my son had developed ADHD and disruptive behavior disorder, that he was depressed, and possibly suicidal. Educators telling me that he would end up being taken from me if I didn't do something, that he would not do well in school and eventually end up in prison. I remember asking God, what did I do wrong? What have I left undone, what haven't I done? What do you WANT ME TO DO? WHAT IS THIS???!!! In the middle of all of my questions, I heard a voice very clearly say to me, SPEAK!!! My response: Speak WHAT!!?? I again heard SPEAK!!! And I asked again, Speak WHAT, and I heard a third time SPEAK!!! OVER JUDAH!!! So as a mother I had some decisions to make. Do I buckle under the pressure? Do I give up? OR DO I SPEAK??? I decided to SPEAK!!! See the Word of God says "You will have what you say" (Mark 11:24) and it also says "Speak those things that are not as though they were" (Romans 4:16-22). So, like I said, I had a choice to make, Remain Silent or SPEAK OVER MY CHILD!!! Thus #CONFESSIONSOFAMOTHER was born.

#Confessionsofamother is a series of affirmations that I spoke concerning my son over a period of 100+days using Facebook as a platform. They began on May 17th and ended July 29th 2014. I got mad, not at the people that said it, but at the devil!!! AND I decided to change my perception of everything negative that had been spoken and done to my child. I began to see these things not as a problem, but an OPPROTUNITY!!!! An opportunity to trust God enough to know that when I speak, and believe what I'm SPEAK-ING THEY WILL MANIFEST!!! That those negative things would not take root in him and he act out what these people have said he was or was going to become. I TOOK AUTHORITY WITH MY MOUTH and SPOKE LIFE over, IN and CONCERNING my child, TO MY CHILD!! After confessing over your child daily, My prayer is that these Confessions empower the reader to take authority over anything thing that would be foolish enough to come up against your seed and see this for what it is an; ANNOUNCE-MENT of the GREATNESS that resides on the inside of your child.

#confessionsofamother...

CONFESSION # 1

SPEAK IT:
My child is blessed and Favored by God. Every curse that has ever been spoken over, about or regarding them is broken by the Power of Jesus Christ.

#confessionsofamother...

CONFESSION #2

SPEAK IT:
My child will graduate top of their class and attend one of the most prestigious universities in the world of their choice.

CONFESSION #3

SPEAK IT:
My child will marry the man/woman God designed for them, the first time; they will NEVER experience divorce or having children outside of marriage. A LONG HAPPY MARRIAGE!!!

CONFESSION #4

SPEAK IT:
My child will not experience the hardship of living paycheck to paycheck. They will walk in abundance and overflow.

#confessionsofamother...

CONFESSION #5

SPEAK IT:
My child will stand in the presence of great men and women

CONFESSION #6

SPEAK IT:
My child is the best combination of his wonderful father and I, and God is going to use this combination to and for His Glory.

#confessionsofamother...

CONFESSION #7

SPEAKI IT:
Let the mind of Christ also be in my child

#confessionsofamother...

CONFESSION #8

SPEAK IT:
My child will not be a prophecy chaser; they will know God's voice FOR their SELF

#confessionsofamother...

CONFESSION #9

SPEAK IT:
My child will know and understand that it is their God that enables them to OVERCOME!!!

#confessionsofamother...

CONFESSION #10

SPEAK IT:
My child will not be a victim of violence. They will not be a part of any gang, violent, or illegal organization

#confessionsofamother...

CONFESSION #11

SPEAK IT:
My child is a master strategists and problem solver

#confessionsofamother...

CONFESSION #12

SPEAK IT:
My child is filled with compassion and the Love of Christ.

CONFESSION #13

SPEAK IT:
My child will not fall into the trap of religion, but will have a solid and firm relationship with his Lord and Savior.

#confessionsofamother...

CONFESSION #14

SPEAK IT:
My child will NOT experience having an identity crisis, he will be taught to embrace who he truly is...AND LOVE IT!!! FLAWS AND ALL!!!

CONFESSION #15

SPEAK IT:
My child is the apple of God's eye, the called and the chosen of the Most High God

CONFESSION #16

SPEAK IT:
My child walks in divine favor and will continue to ALL THE DAYS OF THEIR LIFE

#confessionsofamother...

CONFESSION #17

SPEAK IT:
My child will NOT have a judgmental spirit, but they are FILLED WITH THE LOVE OF CHRIST.

CONFESSION #18

SPEAK IT:
My child has one of the most brilliant business minds in the earth.

CONFESSION #19

SPEAK IT:
"My child will NEVER experience homelessness and poverty"

#confessionsofamother...

CONFESSION #20

SPEAK IT:
The blessings of the Lord will make my child rich and add NO SORROW TO THEM!!!!

#confessionsofamother...

CONFESSION #21

SPEAK IT:
My child is filled with God's love and forgiveness

CONFESSION # 22

SPEAK IT:
My child is honest and will grow to become a honest adult

#confessionsofamother...

CONFESSION #23

SPEAK IT:
Every dream that is in my child's heart, every godly desire will be accomplished and manifested.

CONFESSION #24

SPEAK IT:
My child will make a POSITIVE mark in the earth.

#confessionsofamother...

CONFESSION #25

SPEAK IT:
My child does NOT suffer from low self- esteem or lack of self
-worth because of life's Situations, they know that ALL things are
working together for their good.

CONFESSION #26

SPEAK IT:
Every generational curse in my child's bloodline is BROKEN.

#confessionsofamother...

CONFESSION #27

SPEAK IT:
God will make my child's name GREAT!!!

CONFESSION #28

SPEAK IT:
My child will be favored and the blessed in area of business. They will be a successful business owner.

#confessionsofamother...

CONFESSION #29

SPEAK IT:
My child is a glory carrier

CONFESSION #30

SPEAK IT:

My child is stable and confident

CONFESSION #31

SPEAK IT:
Father I thank you that ALL things are working together for my child's good

#confessionsofamother...

CONFESSION #32

SPEAK IT:
My child is BLESSED

#confessionsofamother...

CONFESSION #33

SPEAK IT:
Every generational ailment is destroyed over my child's life. They will never suffer from Cancer, Diabetes, Heart Disease, High Blood Pressure, Congestive Heart Failure, Lupus or any other disease that would cause their life to be shorten.

#confessionsofamother...

CONFESSION #34

SPEAK IT:
My child will be wise and cautious concerning their health and healthy living

#confessionsofamother...

CONFESSION #35

SPEAK IT:
My child will NEVER be a beggar

CONFESSION #36

SPEAK IT:
My child will NEVER SEE THE INSIDE OF A PRISON CELL....
NEVER

#confessionsofamother...

CONFESSION #37

SPEAK IT:
My son/ my daughter will be a GREAT father/mother to their children. ALL OF THEIR BABIES WILL HAVE THE SAME FATHER/MOTHER WHICH WILL BE THEIR ONLY HUS-BAND/WIFE.

CONFESSIONS #38

SPEAK IT:
Every learning disability that has been spoken over my child is cancelled and dissolved in the Name of Jesus

CONFESSION #39

SPEAK IT:
My child will accomplish EVERYTHING they were born to accomplish.

CONFESSION#40

SPEAK IT:
My child will NEVER suffering from any form of CANCER. The genetic curse of cancer is broken over is their life and the lives of their children.

CONFESSION #41

SPEAK IT:
My child will NEVER suffering from an addiction to drugs of any kind.

CONFESSION #42

SPEAKI IT:
My child will never suffer from an addiction to sex or pornography; I decree that the love inside of them will not awaken until God's appointed time.

CONFESSION #43

SPEAK IT:
My child will NEVER experience being violated sexually, emotional, or physically. I HIDE THEM from every child molester, every abuser and every user, In the Name of Jesus.

CONFESSION #44

SPEAK IT:
I pray for the wife of my son/for the husband of my daughter, that they are kept, whole, and secure, that they are blessed, and untouched, that they are raised in the fear of God, that they never experiences lack, violation, or sickness, that they are complete in God and have been exposed to their purpose early in life.

#confessionsofamother...

CONFESSION #45

SPEAK IT:
My child will walk in purpose all the days of their life

CONFESSION #46

SPEAK IT:
My child perceives God as He truly is and adopts the teachings of Christ... Simply put, that he's able to love without restraint and forgive without conditions.

#confessionsofamother...

CONFESSION #47

SPEAK IT:
My child will not have ONLY the appearance of holiness, they will
have POWER and there won't be NO denying it...

CONFESSION #48

SPEAK IT:
My child will NEVER experience an addiction to alcohol; they will be and remain sober-minded

#confessionsofamother...

CONFESSION #49

SPEAK IT:
Blessings and not curses over my child's life...

CONFESSION #50

SPEAK IT:
My child is healed... In the Name of Jesus

#confessionsofamother...

CONFESSION #51

SPEAK IT:
My child is an honor roll student.

#confessionsofamother...

CONFESSION #52

SPEAK IT:
My child is being taught that power of prayer and this will enable them to successfully fight some of life's hardest battles and WIN!!!

CONFESSION #53

SPEAK IT:
My child will grow in faith and will be known for his unwavering faith in his God.

CONFESSION #54

SPEAK IT:
My child is saved, anointed and filled with the Spirit of the Living God

#confessionsofamother...

CONFESSION #55

SPEAK IT:
My child will excel in the area of education, DR....!!!!

#confessionsofamother...

CONFESSION #56

SPEAK IT:
No weapon formed against my child shall be able to prosper and EVERY tongue that rises against them in judgment, shall be condemn!!!

CONFESSION #57

SPEAK IT:
My child can and will overcome EVERY obstacle that he's faced with.

#confessionsofamother...

CONFESSION #58

SPEAK IT:
I have an amazing child

#confessionsofamother...

CONFESSION #59

SPEAK IT:
My child is gifted

CONFESSION #60

SPEAK IT:
My child is not promiscuous; they will not run from person to person looking for love.

#confessionsofamother...

CONFESSION #61

SPEAK IT:
Every void in my child's life is filled

CONFESSION #62

SPEAK IT:
My child will live their lives to the fullest and have no regrets.

CONFESSION #63

SPEAK IT:
My child does not and will not suffer from suicide, depression or any other mental illness. That curse is broken over his life and in his blood line.

CONFESSION #64

SPEAK IT:
My child has and will have the right friends that will help him grow and stay on the right path.

CONFESSION #65

SPEAK IT:
My child is grateful and appreciative for what God has done for them through others.

CONFESSION #66

SPEAK IT:
My child does not and will not suffer from anxiety which produces panic attacks and other physical ailments.

#confessionsofamother...

CONFESSION #67

SPEAK IT:
My child will be a great judge of character and not a judge of mistakes.

CONFESSION #68

SPEAK IT:
My child has creative mind and an amazing imagination.

#confessionsofamother...

CONFESSION #69

SPEAK IT:
My child is not limited by what they see; they know that beyond the sky is not a limit!!

CONFESSION #70

SPEAK IT:
My child can do all things through Christ which strengthens them.

#confessionsofamother...

CONFESSION #71

SPEAK IT:
My child will experience the goodness of the Lord while they are in the land of the living.

CONFESSION #72

SPEAK IT:
My child will be a resource in their community, not a destroyer of the community.

#confessionsofamother...

CONFESSION #73

SPEAK IT:
My child is a conduit of peace. They will promote peace and not violence

CONFESION #74

SPEAK IT:
God has a plan and a purpose for my child.

#confessionsofamother...

CONFESSION #75

SPEAK IT:
My child will be a man/woman of wisdom that surpasses their years.

#confessionsofamother...

CONFESSION #76

SPEAK IT:
My child is not lazy, they are a hardworking. They are not pro-crastinators.

#confessionsofamother...

CONFESSION #77

SPEAK IT:
My child will not make excuses for their mistakes; they will learn from them and make better decisions.

CONFESSION #78

SPEAK IT:
My child will not be a user or an abuser. They will value and respect people.

#confessionsofamother...

CONFESSION #79

SPEAK IT:
My child is not a thief. They will NOT steal from their family, friends or strangers. They understand the ideals of hard work and earning what you want.

#confessionsofamother...

CONFESSION #80

SPEAK IT:
My child is not and will not be a gossiper; my child will not be a spreader of rumors and lies. My child will speak life to everyone they meet, be a dismantler of rumors and speak truth in love wherever they go.

#confessionsofamother...

CONFESSION #81

SPEAK IT:
My child will be trustworthy and have integrity.

CONFESSION #82

SPEAK IT:
My child is not a murderer. They will not kill people or their reputations.

CONFESSION #83

SPEAK IT:
My child will have great credit and be a good steward over their finances.

#confessionsofamother...

CONFESSION #84

SPEAK IT:
My child will not be a recipient of welfare or state assistance.

#confessionsofamother...

CONFESSION #85

SPEAK IT:
My child will own land and property.

#confessionsofamother...

CONFESSION #86

SPEAK IT:
My child has and will continue to have healthy relationships.

#confessionsofamother...

CONFESSION #87

SPEAK IT:
My child is a positive influence on those around him.

CONFESSION #88

SPEAK IT:
My child is a leader and not a follower.

#confessionsofamother...

CONFESSION #89

SPEAK IT:
My child believes that miracles can happen EVERYDAY!!!

CONFESSION #90

SPEAK IT:
My child is able to learn and apply what they have learned.

#confessionsofamother...

CONFESSION #91

SPEAK IT:
My child is a WINNER!!!!

CONFESSION #92

SPEAK IT:
My child has and will have healthy habits that will ensure a successful, happy and healthy life.

#confessionsofamother...

CONFESSION #93

SPEAK IT:
My child is fearless and brave. They believe that there is nothing they can not accomplish.

CONFESSION #94

SPEAK IT:
My child is not jealous or envious of anyone.

#confessionsofamother...

CONFESSION #95

SPEAK IT:
My child is going to continue to make me a proud mother.

#confessionsofamother...

CONFESSION #96

SPEAK IT:
My child's perception of life is and remains positive.

#confessionsofamother...

CONFESSION #97

SPEAK IT:
Today marks the beginning of the BEST YEARS OF my child's life...

CONFESSION #98

SPEAK IT:
My child is GREAT...

#confessionsofamother...

CONFESSION #99

SPEAK IT:
My child is cover and protected by the Blood of Jesus and no EVIL thing will be able to come near them.

CONFESSION #100

SPEAK IT:
And because I have learned to speak well of my child, they have learned to speak well of themselves.

#confessionsofamother...

After speaking over, to and concerning my son, He has learned to speak well of himself. This last confession is what my son spoke over HIM SELF!!!

**CONFESSION #101 – JUDAH'S CONFESSION
I WILL BE ON PRINCIPAL'S HONOR ROLL THIS YEAR... I agree with Judah, He will be on Principal's honor roll this year. #confessionsofamother and Judah**

"Because you have spoke well of them, they have learned to speak well of them- selves"

ISW

www.ingramcontent.com/pod-product-compliance
Lightning Source LLC
LaVergne TN
LVHW021402080426
835508LV00020B/2416